For My

Daughter

on Her

Wedding Day

For My Daughter on Her Wedding Day

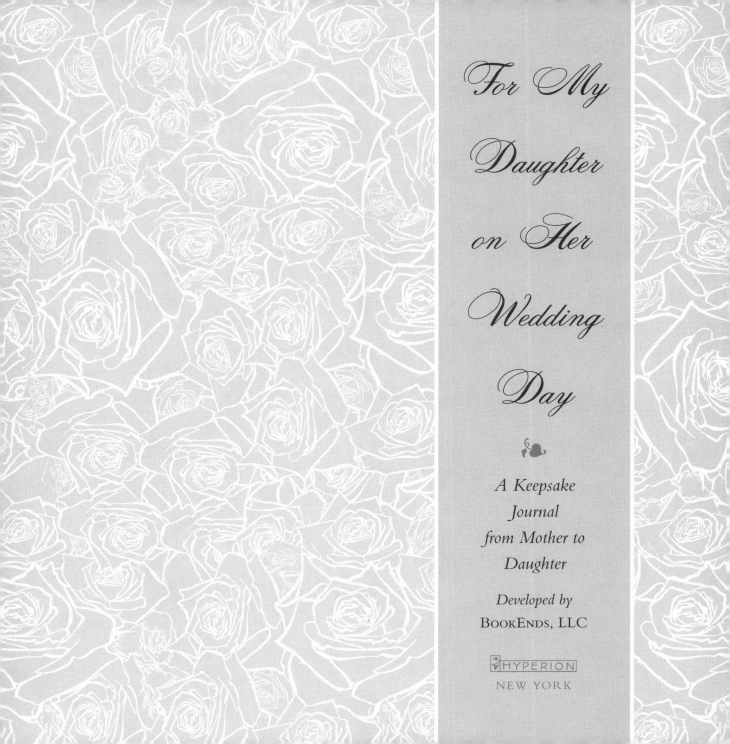

A Keepsake Journal from Mother to Daughter

Developed by
BookEnds, LLC

HYPERION

NEW YORK

Book design by Ruth Lee

Library of Congress Cataloging-in-Publication Data

For my daughter on her wedding day : a keepsake journal from mother to
    daughter.—1st ed.
        p. cm.
    ISBN: 0-7868-6681-0
    1. Bridal books. 2. Weddings—Miscellanea. 3. Mothers—Diaries.

HQ746.F67 2001
306.874'3—dc21

00-044966

FIRST EDITION

10   9   8   7   6   5   4   3   2   1

I want you to have this very special book because . . .

....

....

....

....

....

....

....

....

....

....

The relationship between a mother and a daughter is something that no one—outside of another mother and daughter—will ever truly understand. It is one of love, deep friendship, and admiration. At the same time, this relationship is made up of two people who are often too much alike, too entirely different, too proud, and too embarrassed of each other all at once.

Your mother is someone who is always there for you. She makes you chicken soup when you are sick, holds your hand when you are scared, and dries your tears when you are sad. She is the only person you can trust to always tell the truth . . . even if you don't want to hear it. And there is no one like a mother to share your greatest happinesses with. She will always be there, watching your life story unfold, watching you change from a dependent little girl into a powerful, mature woman. And as the major rites of passage come upon you in life, she will support you, love you, and witness your changes.

While a wedding is truly about the bride and groom and the once-in-a-lifetime love they have found in each other, it is also between the bride and her mother. Every little girl envisions what her wedding will be like and every mother imagines what her daughter will look like when she walks down the aisle.

Not only is a wedding a time of friendship, love, laughter, and even fighting between a mother and a daughter, it is also a time for them to share their hopes and fears of the future and the stories of the past.

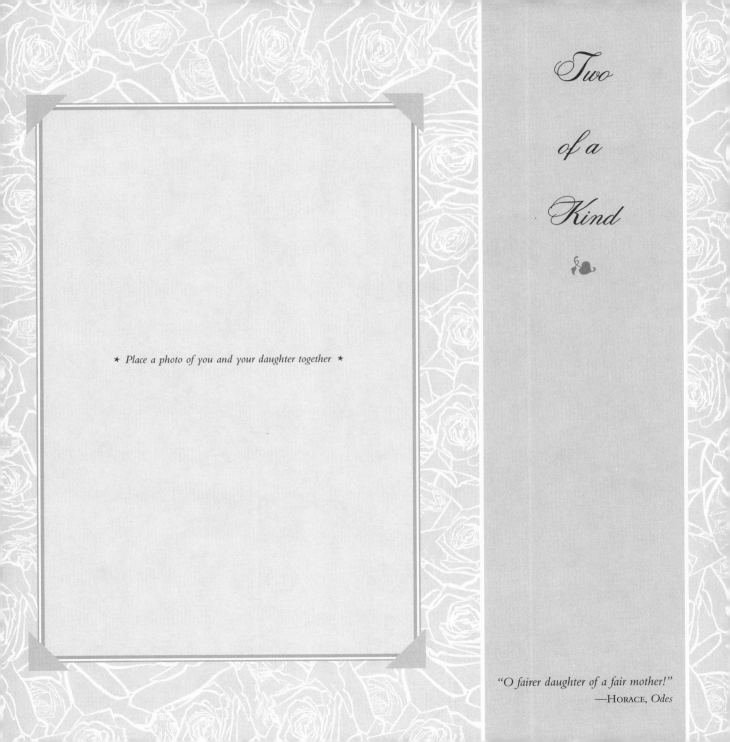

★ Place a photo of you and your daughter together ★

Two
of a
Kind

"O fairer daughter of a fair mother!"
—Horace, *Odes*

Mother,

Daughter,

Best Friends

*"A mother is the truest friend we
   have, when trials, heavy and sudden,
   fall upon us;
When adversity takes the place of
   prosperity;
When friends who rejoice with us in
   our sunshine, desert us;
When troubles thicken around us, still
   will she cling to us,
And endeavor by her kind precepts and
   counsels to dissipate the clouds of
   darkness,
And cause peace to return to our
   hearts."*

—WASHINGTON IRVING

You are both daughter and best friend to me because . . .

I think our relationship is special because . . .

....
....
....
....
....
....
....
....
....
....
....
....
....
....
....
....
....
....
....
....
....
....
....
....
....

"We cannot really love anybody with whom we never laugh."
—AGNES REPPLIER

Like Mother, Like Daughter

I think you are most like me because . . .

....
....
....
....
....
....
....
....
....
....

I think you are least like me because . . .

....
....
....
....
....
....
....
....
....
....
....
....
....

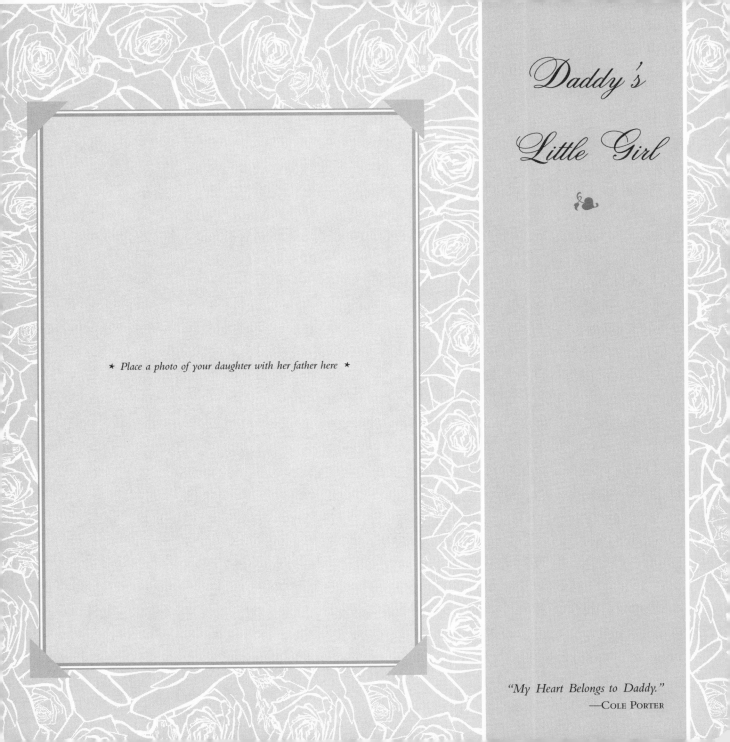

★ Place a photo of your daughter with her father here ★

Daddy's
Little Girl

"My Heart Belongs to Daddy."
—Cole Porter

How I think you are most like your father:

....
....
....
....
....
....
....
....
....
....
....
....
....
....
....
....
....
....
....
....
....
....
....
....

How I think you are least like your father:

Characteristics you have that are distinctly you:

....

....

....

....

....

....

....

....

....

....

....

....

....

....

....

....

....

....

....

....

....

....

....

....

....

....

....

When I think of you as a little girl, I always remember you as . . .

....

....

....

....

....

....

....

....

....

....

....

....

....

....

....

....

....

....

....

....

....

....

....

"What are little girls made of?
Sugar and spice, and everything nice;
That's what little girls are made of."
—CHILDREN'S NURSERY RHYME

I'll never forget the time that you . . .

....
....
....
....
....
....
....
....
....
....
....

It was special to me because . . .

....
....
....
....
....
....
....
....
....
....
....

*"We can do no great things; only
small things with great love."*
—MOTHER TERESA

I've never been more proud of you than when . . .

"My father would have enjoyed what you have so generously said of me—and my mother would have believed it."

—LYNDON B. JOHNSON

You made me laugh when you . . .

....

....

....

....

....

....

....

....

....

....

....

You made me cry when you . . .

....

....

....

....

....

....

....

....

....

....

....

*"Love comforteth like
sunshine after rain."*
—WILLIAM SHAKESPEARE

I'll never forget the time when we . . .

....

....

....

....

....

....

....

....

....

....

....

....

....

....

....

....

....

....

....

....

....

....

....

*Special times between a mother
and daughter should always be
cherished and remembered.*

Sunny Days

These days stand out particularly in my memory as very special days for us:

....
....
....
....
....
....
....
....
....
....
....
....
....
....
....
....
....
....
....
....
....
....
....
....
....
....

I love you so much because . . .

....

....

....

....

....

....

....

....

....

....

....

....

....

....

....

....

....

....

....

....

....

A

Mother's

Love

"To love someone deeply gives you strength.
Being loved by someone deeply gives you courage."

—Lao Tzu

You frustrate me most when you . . .

I knew that you were no longer a little girl when . . .

You have become a woman I'm proud to know because . . .

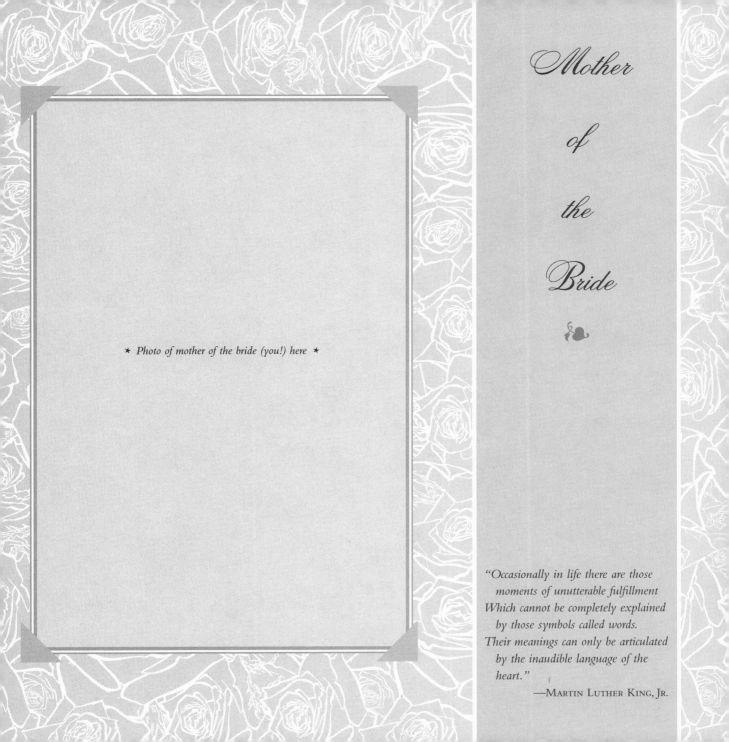

★ Photo of mother of the bride (you!) here ★

Mother

of

the

Bride

"Occasionally in life there are those moments of unutterable fulfillment Which cannot be completely explained by those symbols called words. Their meanings can only be articulated by the inaudible language of the heart."

—MARTIN LUTHER KING, JR.

Who Gives This Woman?

"Blessed is the influence of one true, loving human soul on another."
—George Eliot

The day you told me you were getting married, I thought . . .

I said . . .

I felt . . .

I immediately told . . .

And they said . . .

I'm most excited about your wedding because . . .

Being the mother of the bride makes me feel . . .

....
....
....
....
....
....
....
....
....
....
....
....
....
....
....
....
....
....
....
....
....
....
....
....
....
....

"Joy is the feeling of grinning on the inside."

—DR. MELBA COLGROVE

Meeting Mr. Right

"Two souls with but a single thought,
Two hearts that beat as one."

—Freidrich Halm

I knew you had met the man of your dreams when . . .

....

....

....

....

....

....

....

....

....

....

....

....

....

....

....

....

....

....

....

....

....

....

The first time I met your fiancé, I thought . . .

I think your fiancé is perfect for you because . . .

....

....

....

....

....

....

....

....

....

....

....

....

....

....

....

....

....

....

....

....

....

....

....

....

....

"The prudence of the best heads is often
Defeated by tenderness of the best hearts."
—HENRY FIELDING

I like my future son-in-law because . . .

....

....

....

....

....

....

....

....

....

....

....

....

....

....

....

....

....

....

....

....

....

....

"True, we love life, not because we
are used to living,
But because we are used to loving.
There is always some madness in
love,
But there is also always some reason
in madness."
—FRIEDRICH NIETZSCHE

I think you make the perfect couple because . . .

I know that you will have a good marriage because . . .

Memory Lane

★ Engagement or wedding photo of you and your husband ★

*"There is only one happiness in life,
to love and be loved."*

—George Sand

Your father and I met . . .

....
....
....
......:...
....
....
....
....
....
....
....
....
....
....
....
....
....
....
....
....
....
....
....
....

A

Great

Romance

"I have more memories than if I were a thousand years old."

—CHARLES BAUDELAIRE

Our first date . . .

I thought your father was special because . . .

I knew I loved your father when . . .

He asked me to marry him . . .

I said . . .

"We can only learn to love by loving."
—IRIS MURDOCH

35

I felt . . .

....
....
....
....
....
....
....
....
....
....
....

We were engaged for (how long) . . .

....
....
....
....
....
....
....
....
....
....
....
....

Our parents (your grandparents) reacted . . .

....
....
....
....
....
....
....
....
....
....
....
....

My parents . . .

....
....
....
....
....
....
....
....
....
....
....
....

His parents . . .

Our engagement was . . .

....
....
....
....
....
....
....
....
....
....
....
....
....
....
....
....
....
....
....
....
....
....
....
....

The things we did, the things we said.
Those last days of being single and the first days of being in love.
An engagement can seem endless or go too fast.
It can be frightening, and wonderful all at the same time.

How your wedding compares to/differs from mine:

❧ My dress was . . .   While yours is . . .

....
....
....
....

❧ What I loved most about my   What I love about yours is . . .
   dress was . . .

....
....
....
....

❧ Your dad wore . . .   While your groom is wearing . . .

....
....
....
....

❧ My flowers were . . .   While yours are . . .

....
....
....
....

🐚 My reception was . . .   While yours is . . .

....
....
....
....

🐚 Mine cost . . .   While yours costs . . .

....
....
....
....

🐚 My ceremony was . . .   While yours is . . .

....
....
....
....

🐚 My cake was . . .   While yours is . . .

....
....
....
....

❧ My food was . . .   While yours is . . .

....
....
....
....

❧ My music was . . .   While yours is . . .

....
....
....
....

❧ I was _____ years old.   You are _____.

....
....
....
....

❧ Our honeymoon was . . .   While yours will be . . .

....
....
....
....

Other differences between our weddings are . . .

Things about your wedding that are very similar to mine are . . .

Weddings sure have changed over the years.

Things you are doing that no one ever did in my day are . . .

....

....

....

....

....

....

....

....

....

....

....

....

....

....

....

....

....

....

....

....

The

Changes

of

Time

"Everything flows and nothing stays . . .
You can't step twice into the same river."

—HERACLITUS

My attendants were:

....

....

....

....

....

....

....

I chose them because . . .

....

....

....

....

....

....

....

They wore . . .

....

....

....

....

....

....

....

"I dreamed of a wedding of elaborate elegance;
A church filled with flowers and friends.
I asked him what kind of wedding he wished for;
He said one that would make me his wife."

—SOURCE UNKNOWN

Your father's attendants were:

....

....

....

....

....

....

....

....

....

....

....

He chose them because . . .

....

....

....

....

....

....

....

....

....

....

....

Other special people in our wedding were:

....
....
....
....
....
....
....
....
....
....
....

Guests at our wedding included . . .

....
....
....
....
....
....
....
....
....
....
....

"Friendship is Love without his wings!"

—LORD BYRON

These are the friends, family, and loved ones who made our day all the more special.

★ *Place a photo of your wedding party here* ★

Don't forget to write who's who below!!

There we are! From left to right:

Picture

Perfect

If I had to do my wedding over again, I would . . .

This is what the night before the wedding was like for me:

....

....

....

....

....

....

....

....

....

This is what I did the morning of the wedding:

....

....

....

....

....

....

....

....

....

....

Get

Ready . . .

Get

Set . . .

This is how I felt the day of my wedding:

....
....
....
....
....
....
....
....
....
....

If I could do it over, I'd do this the morning of the wedding:

....
....
....
....
....
....
....
....
....
....
....
....

My fondest memory from my wedding is . . .

....

....

....

....

....

....

....

....

....

....

....

....

....

....

....

....

....

....

....

....

....

....

....

....

Sweet

Memories

*"When to the sessions of sweet silent thought
I summon up remembrance of things past."*

—WILLIAM SHAKESPEARE

Something

Old

Special keepsakes I have saved from my wedding:

....

....

....

....

....

....

....

....

....

....

They are special to me because . . .

....

....

....

....

....

....

....

....

....

....

....

....

My most memorable wedding gift:

....
....
....
....
....
....
....
....
....
....
....
....

My most ridiculous gift:

....
....
....
....
....
....
....
....
....
....
....
....

The advice my mother gave me on my wedding day was . . .

....

....

....

....

....

....

....

....

....

....

....

....

....

....

....

....

....

....

....

....

....

....

....

*"A word spoken in due season,
how good it is!"*
—THE HOLY BIBLE: PROVERBS

My bridal shower was thrown by these people:

....
....
....
....
....
....
....
....

My favorite memories from my shower are . . .

....
....
....
....
....
....
....
....
....
....

Shower

Me

with

Love

The first bridal shower was about 300
years ago in Holland.
The story says that a Dutch maiden
fell in love with a penniless man
And her father refused to give her
money to marry her love.
In honor of true love, her friends and
neighbors got together to give
The maiden everything she needed to
start her new life.

Favorite memories from our honeymoon are . . .

....
....
....
....
....
....
....
....
....
....
....
....
....
....
....
....
....
....
....
....
....
....
....

*"The best thing about traveling
is going home."*
—CHARLES DUDLEY WARNER

★ *Place a picture from your daughter's wedding here* ★

Your

Special

Day

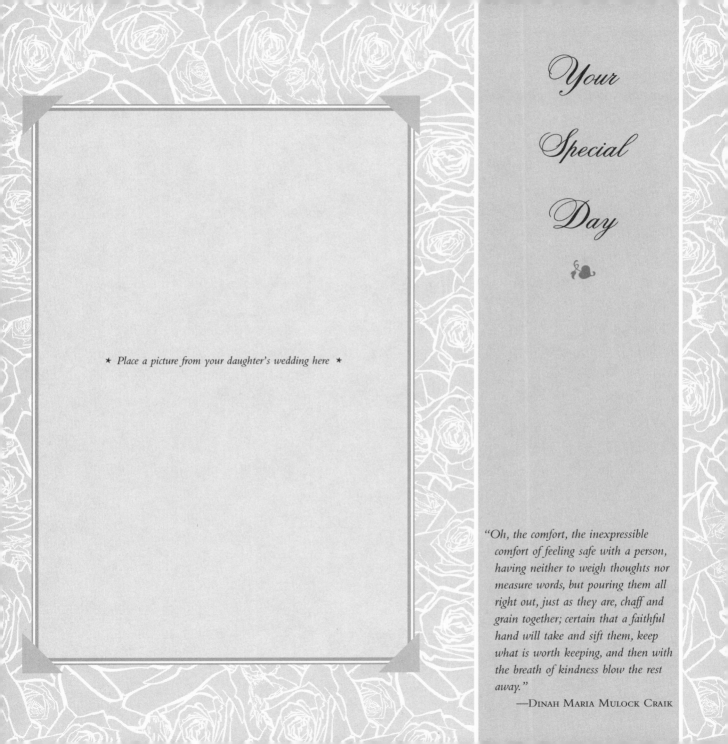

"Oh, the comfort, the inexpressible comfort of feeling safe with a person, having neither to weigh thoughts nor measure words, but pouring them all right out, just as they are, chaff and grain together; certain that a faithful hand will take and sift them, keep what is worth keeping, and then with the breath of kindness blow the rest away."

—DINAH MARIA MULOCK CRAIK

Of all your wedding plans, I am most excited about . . .

....
....
....
....
....
....
....
....
....
....
....
....
....
....
....
....
....
....
....
....
....
....
....
....
....
....
....

*"He who chooses the beginning of a
road chooses the place it leads to.
It is the means that determine the
end."*

—HARRY EMERSON FOSDICK

Wedding plans that I think sound most like you are . . .

....
....
....
....
....
....
....
....
....
....
....
....
....
....
....
....
....
....
....
....
....
....
....

"All great deeds and all great thoughts have a ridiculous beginning.
Great works are often born on a street corner or in a restaurant's revolving door."
—ALBERT CAMUS

You

Always

Surprise

Me

❧

" 'Curiouser and curiouser!'
cried Alice."
—LEWIS CARROLL

I was surprised when you told me you wanted to . . .

....
....
....
....
....
....
....
....
....

Because . . .

....
....
....
....
....
....
....
....
....
....

Something I would like you to have/wear on your wedding day is . . .

....
....
....
....
....
....
....
....
....
....
....
....
....
....
....
....
....
....

Something

Old,

Something

Borrowed

*Something Old . . . Something
New . . .
Something Borrowed . . . Something
Blue . . .
And a Sixpence in Your Shoe*

It means so much to me because . . .

When you were a little girl, I always imagined your wedding . . .

Listen

to

Your

Mother

My advice on your wedding day is . . .

I would recommend these gifts for your registry (things I think you can't live without!):

....

....

....

....

....

....

....

....

....

....

....

....

....

....

....

....

....

....

....

....

....

....

....

....

....

....

Things you are registering for that make me laugh:

....

....

....

....

....

....

....

Items that I don't think you'll ever use:

....

....

....

....

....

....

....

Gifts that are so "you":

....

....

....

....

....

....

....

When all is going on around you and you are in the midst of your very special day, make sure to take time out to . . .

....
....
....
....
....
....
....
....
....
....
....
....
....
....
....
....
....
....
....
....
....
....
....
....

"God gave us memory so that we might have roses in December."
—SIR JAMES. M. BARRIE

Family Affair

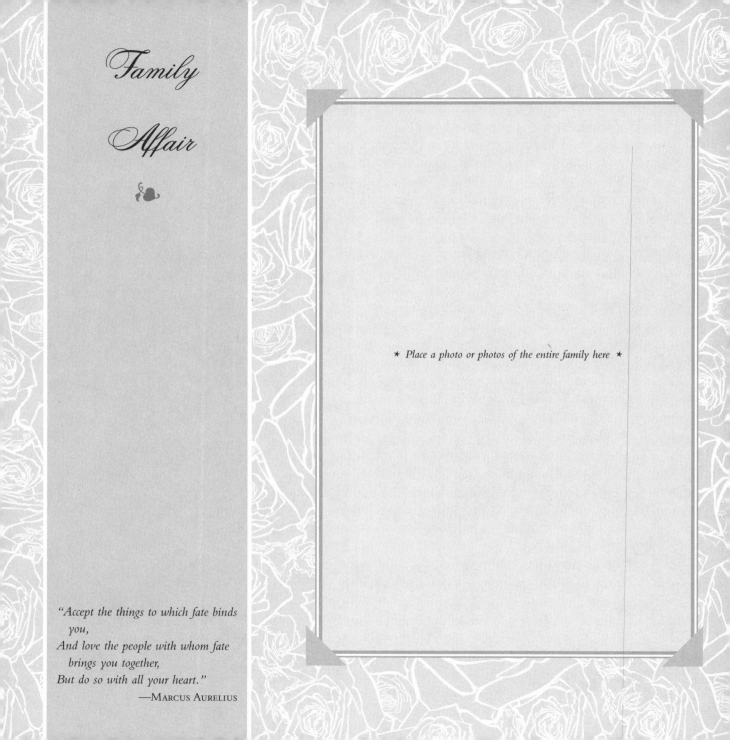

★ *Place a photo or photos of the entire family here* ★

"Accept the things to which fate binds you,
And love the people with whom fate brings you together,
But do so with all your heart."
—Marcus Aurelius

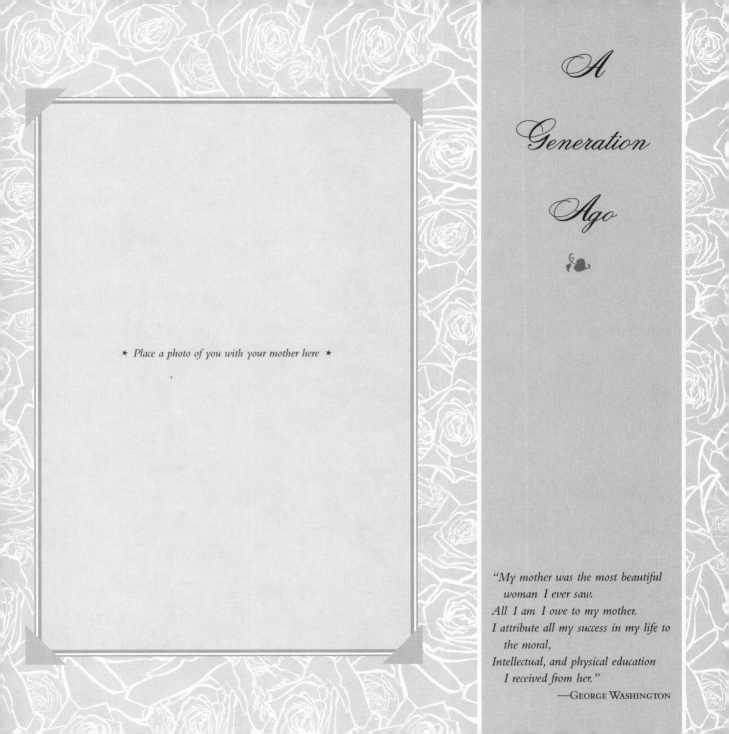

★ *Place a photo of you with your mother here* ★

A Generation Ago

"My mother was the most beautiful woman I ever saw.
All I am I owe to my mother.
I attribute all my success in my life to the moral,
Intellectual, and physical education I received from her."
—GEORGE WASHINGTON

My relationship with my own mother was . . .

Some of my favorite memories of my mother are . . .

....
....
....
....
....
....
....
....
....
....
....
....
....
....
....
....
....
....
....
....
....
....
....
....

*"The best and most beautiful things
in the world cannot be seen,
Nor touched . . . but are felt in the
heart."*
—HELEN KELLER

You remind me of my mother when you . . .

Some things my mother taught me that I'll never forget are . . .

My relationship with my mother-in-law was . . .

....
....
....
....
....
....
....
....
....
....
....
....
....
....
....
....
....
....
....
....
....
....
....
....

In Bohemia it is a custom for the
bride's mother-in-law
to greet the bride outside her house
the morning of the wedding
with a cup of coffee or a glass of
wine.
After drinking it, the bride tosses the
glass over her shoulder;
it is considered good luck if the glass
does not break.

Special memories of my mother-in-law are . . .

You remind me of my mother-in-law when you . . .

....

....

....

....

....

....

....

....

....

....

....

....

....

....

....

....

....

....

....

....

....

....

....

....

....

*"We don't love qualities; we love a
person;
Sometimes by reason of their defects
as well as their qualities."*
—JACQUES MARITAIN

Advice I'd give on mothers-in-law . . .

My mother-in-law was so different from my mother because . . .

★ *Place a photo of your in-laws (bride's paternal grandparents) here* ★

"Be tolerant of the human race.
Your whole family belongs to it—
And some of your spouse's family does
too."

—Anonymous

When I first met my in-laws (your grandparents), I thought . . .

How my relationship with my in-laws changed over the years:

When I first met my brothers- and sisters-in-law, our relationships were . . .

How our relationships changed over the years:

....

....

....

....

....

....

....

....

....

....

....

....

....

....

....

....

....

....

....

....

....

....

....

....

....

My advice to you on being a great daughter-in-law is . . .

I would like to be the kind of mother-in-law who . . .

Happily Ever After

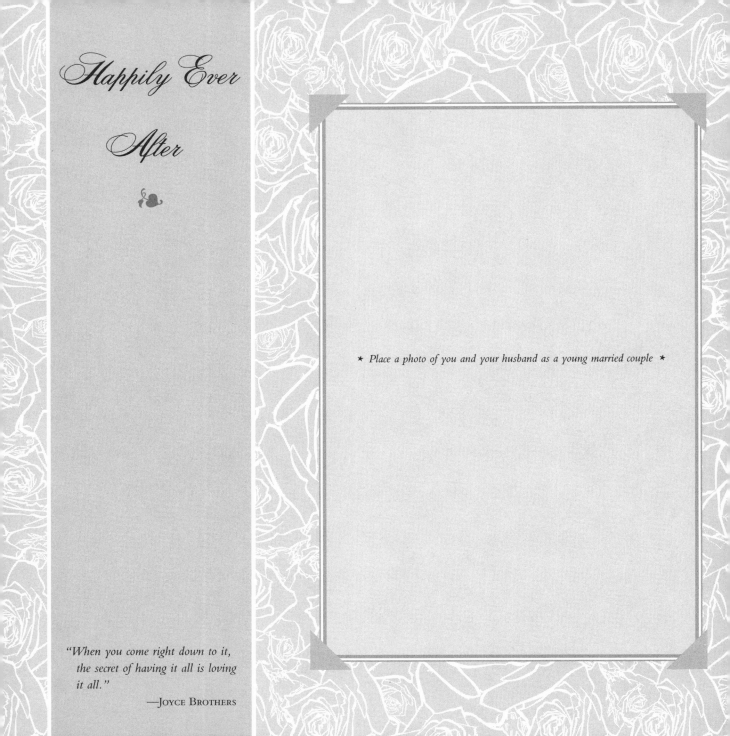

★ *Place a photo of you and your husband as a young married couple* ★

"When you come right down to it, the secret of having it all is loving it all."

—JOYCE BROTHERS

I think the keys to a successful marriage are . . .

....

....

....

....

....

....

....

....

....

....

....

....

....

....

....

....

....

....

....

....

....

....

....

....

....

Mother

Knows Best

"Love is an ideal thing,
Marriage is a real thing;
A confusion of the real with the ideal
never goes unpunished."
—JOHANN WOLFGANG VON GOETHE

Advice my mother gave me on marriage . . .

- Always say you're sorry.
- The sooner you accept the fact that your husband isn't perfect, the closer you'll be to having a perfect marriage.
- Don't make promises you can't keep.
- Don't hold grudges.

....
....
....
....
....
....
....
....
....
....
....
....
....
....
....
....
....
....
....
....
....

*"People need loving the most
When they deserve it the least."*
—JOHN HARRIGAN

Memories of my first days of marriage are . . .

> The first time someone called me Mrs.
> Eating breakfast together.
> Moving in together.
> Cooking dinner.

....

....

....

....

....

....

When we were first married, we lived . . .

....

....

....

....

....

....

....

....

....

....

....

Welcome,

Mrs. . . .

A typical day or week for me was . . .

On the weekends we used to . . .

....

....

....

....

....

....

....

....

....

....

....

....

....

....

....

....

....

....

....

....

....

....

....

....

"May you live every day of your life."
—Jonathan Swift

Friends we had:

....
....
....
....
....
....
....
....
....
....
....
....
....
....
....
....
....
....
....
....
....
....
....
....

*"I count myself in nothing else so
    happy
As in a soul remembering my good
    friends."*
          —WILLIAM SHAKESPEARE

Life was wonderful because . . .

....
....
....
....
....
....
....
....
....
....
....
....
....
....
....
....
....
....
....
....
....
....
....
....

*"There is nothing nobler or more
    admirable
Than when two people who see eye
    to eye
Keep house as man and wife,
Confounding their enemies and
    delighting their friends."*
                    —HOMER, *Odyssey*

Disagreements we had:

....

....

....

....

....

....

....

....

....

....

....

....

....

....

....

....

....

....

....

....

....

....

....

....

....

"The ultimate test of a relationship
Is to disagree but hold hands."
—ALEXANDER PENNEY

Your father made me laugh when he . . .

....

....

....

....

....

....

....

....

....

....

....

....

....

....

....

....

....

....

....

....

....

....

....

....

"The most wasted day is that in which we have not laughed."
—CHAMFORT

Some of my fondest memories of early married life are . . .

Some of the toughest things about being newlyweds were . . .

It took me decades to learn the following wisdom that I'd like you to know now . . .

Things I learned from your father . . .

....
....
....
....
....
....
....
....
....
....

Things I taught your father . . .

....
....
....
....
....
....
....
....
....
....

New Ideas

When two people get married they bring into their marriage new traditions, new ideals, and different ideas of what a family should be.

Household chores and how we divided them up:

🙎 Laundry

....
....
....

🙎 Cleaning

....
....
....

🙎 Taking the garbage out

....
....
....

🙎 Yard work

....
....
....

🙎 Dishes

....
....

🙎 Cooking

....
....
....

🙎 Household repairs

....
....
....

🙎 Keeping track of finances/
budgeting

....
....
....

🙎 Grocery shopping

....
....
....

🙎 Gift buying

....
....

Other chores:

....
....
....
....
....
....
....
....
....
....
....
....

How the division of chores has changed over the years:

....
....
....
....
....
....
....
....
....
....
....
....
....

A Whole

New World

There was a time when traditional wives only had one job, to take care of their husbands. In the modern world I hope that your husband will do more than just look out for you.

"Homemaker is the ultimate career. All other careers exist for one purpose only—
To support the ultimate career."
—C. S. Lewis

I hope your husband will also . . .

I hope you will also . . .

....
....
....
....
....
....
....
....
....
....
....
....
....
....
....
....
....
....
....
....
....
....
....
....
....
....

In the same vein, the duties of a wife have also changed over the years. I hope that you will do more than just cook, clean, and dote on your husband.

Family Traditions

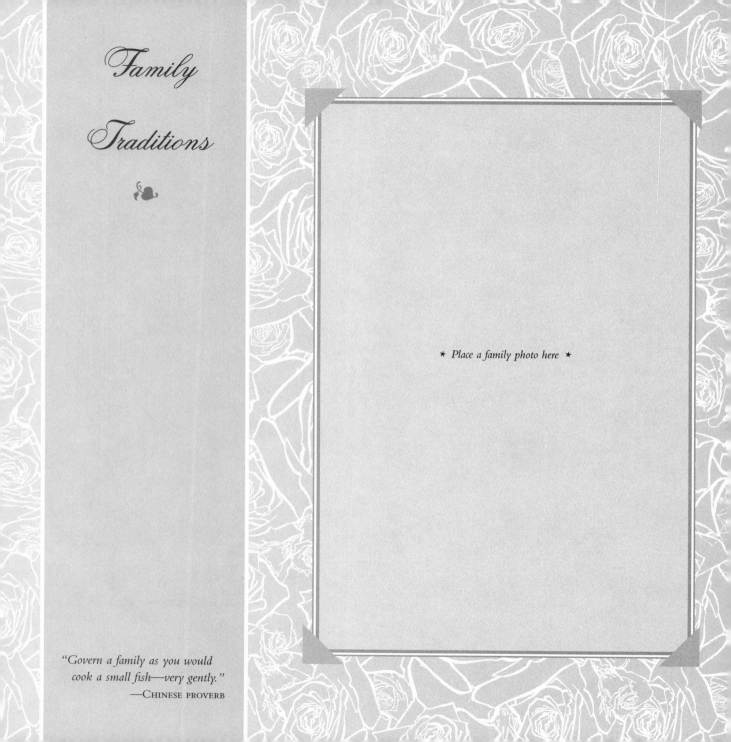

★ *Place a family photo here* ★

"Govern a family as you would cook a small fish—very gently."
—CHINESE PROVERB

Birthday Traditions . . .

....

....

....

....

....

....

....

....

....

....

....

....

....

....

....

....

....

....

*Special
Family
Traditions and
Where They
Came From*

*The words to a favorite birthday song,
a special cake plate, the ornaments
on the Christmas tree, midnight
Mass, Fourth of July picnics, or
May Day baskets . . .*

Holiday Traditions

When thinking of holiday traditions, don't limit yourself to "major" holidays. Remember Grandpa's famous July Fourth picnic, Irish stew dinner on St. Patrick's Day, and the traditional President's Day barbecue.

....

....

....

....

....

....

....

....

....

....

....

....

....

....

....

....

....

....

....

....

....

Family stories are often what makes a family. Whether it is grandma accidentally feeding the Christmas dinner to the dog or the tale of your grandparents and their immigration to the United States, these are the stories that bring a group of people together as a family. These are also the stories that shouldn't be forgotten, but shared with generations to come.

Brief Family History

A family's history is what separates us from the neighbor's family. Take a moment to jot down what countries your family is from, states or cities they have lived in, as well as the history of those now lost to us.

....
....
....
....
....
....
....
....
....
....
....
....
....
....
....
....
....
....
....
....
....
....

Family traditions don't have to mean complicated dinners or special holidays. They could be simple things, like planting a Mother's Day garden, Sunday morning brunch, or a special lullaby sung to babies.

Family

Traditions

I Hope

You

Continue . . .

Family Dinners and Special Recipes

In the Caribbean a rich black cake baked with dried fruits and nuts is a popular wedding dessert. The recipe is embellished as it is handed down from mother to daughter.

Your father's favorite dish:

Your favorite meal as a child:

Your favorite meal as an adult:

....
....
....
....
....
....
....
....
....
....
....
....
....
....
....
....
....
....
....
....
....
....
....

My favorite dessert recipes:

A meal for special occasions:

Recipes my mother passed down to me:

Recipes your father's mother gave me:

Other favorite recipes and why they are special:

....
....
....
....
....
....
....
....
....
....
....
....
....
....
....
....
....
....
....
....
....
....
....
....
....